Advance Praise

Heart of the Prairie is open at all hours in all seasons.
Filled with slice-of-life poems about cow ranching, work,
and small-town living, this seventh book by award-winning
poet Bruce Roseland speaks to life on the Great Plains
"where your good name and word / hold the weight of
your worth." Roseland gives voice to the visceral connection
many South Dakotans have to the land, a tie that sustains
relationships among individuals and communities and
imbues Roseland's poems with a spiritual sense of place.
Not only is this book brimming with bulls and bucks,
coyotes and cottontails, it vibrates with delightful sounds:
"one more chore before snow," "rune-like rock ribbons /
crisscrossing the surface," "mouthed out old cows." In Heart
of the Prairie, rural life is ripe with desire even as it ages,
even as it shifts under the weight of irreversible change.

> – Christine Stewart-Nuñez,
> South Dakota poet laureate

Bruce Roseland's respect and admiration for the life of
those living on the Great Plains in America is evident in the
unique view from a very experienced eye that sees directly
into the heart of the prairie. His collection of poems not
only direct you into the conversations at the local coffee
stop, but serves as a tribute to the Dirty Thirties, the truth
and vivid descriptions, that takes the reader back to the
harsh reality of the struggles had by our predecessors.

> – Yvonne Hollenbeck

i

Nearly a century ago, Robert Frost visited the farm of the Iowa poet/farmer, James Hearst, and, having read some of Hearst's poetry, told him that the words in his poems "had callouses on them." It was a compliment, and it can also be said about Bruce Roseland's poems.

Reading HEART OF THE PRAIRIE reminds me (having read other books by Bruce) that it's one thing to own land and livestock and work hard every day to make a living, but that it's something altogether different and unique to be able to describe and account for that arduous life consistently and prolifically in poems. I see Bruce's special talent as having found a balance between the lived life and the words that describe that life.

Here's a list of just a few features of that balance I'm referring to: "Occupational hazards": in the poem with the same title, the speaker gets a broken neck, "the results of being in the path/ of an occasional cow taking a shortcut,/ the results of choosing not to earn a living/ sitting behind a desk." And in the poem, "Jordan," a neighbor gets run over by a bull . . . "broken vertebrae, said the doc," and then the "opiates knocking back the pain," and the "chills and shakes" in bed, "sweating it out."

Humor/lightness in "Before eharmony," a woman who lost her husband, and, feeling lonely on a windy day, "she tied a note/onto a big tumbleweed/ that said: "Need Company?" And then, "Weeks later, a trail-worn cowboy/ stopped by, tipped his hat/while holding the note in his hand./ She sized him up,/ maybe,/just maybe,/ her shining knight."

"Nature red in tooth and claw": in "Divine right," the tops of "three-quarter-ton-cylinders of hay" are seen as "dining tables" with "Disembodied legs of upland birds . . ." "macabre claws attached to leg sticks" . . . "swept skyward in mid-stride/ by a hawk plying his daily trade . . . ." And here's the short poem, "Dawn's early light": When a rooster crows/ at first light of day,' letting the sun know who's boss,/ he also lets the fox know/ where the chickens are."

Philosophy/wistfulness: in "Finding a Way," the poet watches cow paths and thinks of how they meander, "leading around, not over,/ holes and rocks." Then says that he too is "engaged in work/ that turns nature to my own use./ I cannot stay unless/what I do feeds me./ If you were to follow me/ on many of my days, you would think my path, too, meanders."

Camaraderie: in "Today's town square"—"in country towns/nursing coffees at four-seater/rectangular tables in crossroads gas stops." And the keen insight: "Each time the door opens up, they note who comes and goes."

The hundred-plus pages of *Heart of the Prairie* show Bruce Roseland—tough-minded, physical, sensitive, wise— firing on all of his cylinders. The life and the work together.
– David Allan Evans

Heart of the Prairie is both a necessary call to save a fragile ecosystem, as well as a reminder that poetry can become a type of lyrical memoir. His work captures the daily beauty and hardship of ranching life from the frost of a windless day, to watching a gopher, to finding meadowlarks frozen in a snowbank, to the hard work of having to shoot a sickly bull—'I find myself saying "I'm sorry,"/ as I touch off the rounds.'" Told with a hawk's clear eye and a generous heart, Roseland invites us onto his land, he shows us the wide horizon of decades, and he laments the vanishing grasslands. Heart of the Prairie is a nurturing of words that tells the story of weathered hands tending weathered, beloved, earth.
– Patrick Hicks,
author of *The Commandant of Lubizec, Adoptable,* and *In the Shadow of Dora*

Heart of the Prairie is built of words and phrases that ring with prairie experiences. Bruce Roseland writes about the work of ranchers in this arid grassland, who "keep doing it until they can't." When the land talks to the poet, he listens, perhaps sitting in a red-tail hawk nest atop a haystack. Lamenting the loss of grassland to big agriculture's focus on production, he says it leaves "no room for a bird, for a bee/ for a wild flower or tree." And he understands the truth of "South Dakota nice": if the annual ice-fishing derby can't be held because there's no ice, the officials give away the prizes anyway.

– Linda M. Hasselstrom

A loving, honest tribute to South Dakota's landscapes, people, and history. Heart of the Prairie is both a celebration of days gone by and a roadmap for a better future.

– Stephanie Anderson,
author of *One Size Fits None: A Farm Girl's Search for the Promise of Regenerative Agriculture*

Heart of the Prairie

Bruce Roseland

Scurfpea
Publishing LLC

Cover photograph by Julianne Hanson.
Cover page photograph by Susan Melius.

Scurfpea Publishing llc
P.O. Box 46
Sioux Falls, SD 57101
scurfpeapublishing.com
editor@scurfpeapublishing.com

Contents

Acknowledgments

I would like to thank Julianne Hanson Roseland, my wife, for her dedication in putting this book together and for passionately believing in the power of words. Thanks to my editor, Steve Boint, for his sharp eye, sharp mind and warm heart. I acknowledge you cannot write what you have not known or felt. Therefore I am grateful for all people, creatures and things growing green upon the earth that bless my life. The world I have been given to live in is good.

Introduction to *Heart of the Prairie*

The South Dakota Missouri Coteau region ("coteau" is French, meaning "rolling hills") is a place that has its own unique ecosystem of fertile grasslands, swales and rocky hillsides, a place that has its own sense of community and culture, a place in which I've lived my life.

Southwestern Faulk County is a part of this region, where my great-grandfather was one of the first settlers. My father, at the age of five, walked behind horses doing field work. I too, in my boyhood, have guided work horses feeding cows on a winter day. This is a land that never was densely populated, and has, in recent times, become even more sparsely populated. This depopulation has been occurring in the face of ever-increasing agricultural development. Those of us remaining on the land try to come to terms with the very real paradoxes we find in our environment, an environment that can be rich and productive but is also, in many ways, harsh and unforgiving. If you are looking for an easy way of living, this is not the place.

So why do we remain here? Perhaps, for many of us, it is the spiritual connection we feel with the land itself as we step out our doors and greet each new day, aware that we can still find a sense of the natural order. We all feel a connection that comes from being birthed under a wide and limitless sky, knowing the certainty of *belonging* to **this** place. Our place. When you share your life with the land and with the living things that grow and pause upon it, you either grow to love it or you leave.

Technological advances have increased agricultural production way beyond my great-grandfather's wildest dreams. In doing so, our once familiar landscape and way of life have changed in ways even my father, and at times myself, cannot recognize. There is much good in this progress, but also the loss of native plants, animals, bugs and birds. These advances have also, regrettably, removed many families who have made their living from the land for generations.

There is no easy answer. You need to know what you have before you know what you are losing. You then need to decide what you value, what is worth preserving, what is worth fighting for and what you are willing to do about it.

My hope is by sharing these stories of a prairie, a homeland, you too will come to see its beauty and believe in its powerful, life-giving mystery. I pray you will realize the urgent need to keep our grassland from disappearing, to join in some practical action to preserve the prairie forever.

Home

Make me a prairie
of sweet-smelling grass
stretching from the panhandle of Texas
upward to the Badlands of North Dakota.
Let the wind come sweeping
down these plains in rolling waves
of ripening seed heads,
speckled with wild flowers
more colorful than the rainbow.
Fill the open-air blue sky with sunshine.
Put up high a red tail hawk
circling with outstretched wings.
Let the glittering stars at night
be the only lights.
Make these plains fruitful with birds, butterflies
and wandering creatures of hooves and paws.
Birth a people who choose to live
where every breath of air is clean and free,
where your good name and word
hold the weight of your worth.
Make us a prairie.

In our hearts

The scent of rain on earth.
The last sight of geese in the fall.
The first sight of geese in the spring.
The first gasping breath of a newborn calf.
The warmth of our homes when winter winds blow.
We who grow a living from the land cannot live
without being connected to this sky and to this prairie,
without hearing the song of birds as they give wing,
without feeling life in our every step as we stride through our days.
Still, we lie awake at night worrying
whether ends will meet,
whether the path we have taken will work out,
whether the rain will come,
whether the sun will shine,
whether our will and physical core shall weaken or stay the course.
We have found the good
while dealing with the bad.
We have stayed, when others have left.
Such is the power of our land's beating heart.

The pie

My grandfather married twice
and had two separate batches of kids.
My dad and his brother were of the first batch,
sharing the operation with their father,
each getting a third of production.
The day dawned that their father decided
he needed more in order to raise his second family.
Both my father and his brother had wives and children –
a single place supporting three families, barely.
One day, in the presence of my grandfather,
my father drew in the dust of the ground
a circle. He divided the circle
into three equal parts and said,
"This is the pie. Where shall we cut
to give one piece a bigger slice?"
My grandfather had no answer.
Within a year or so, the three of them
went on their separate ways.
One sold out.
One left.
Only my father stayed.

Grandpa Bill

When asked what he thought the weather would do, he said,
"Only two kinds of people predict the weather –
newcomers & damn fools."
When asked how long a person could feed rye straw, a fodder
with almost no nutritional value, to livestock
(a pertinent question in the drought-stricken 1930's
when little to no feed was to be had),
he replied, "For the rest of their lives"
(until they starve),
then walked away.
One year, Grandpa had a good crop in the making
until a cloud came up
and hail started coming down.
While he stood in the doorway of his big barn,
he pulled out his pocket watch to check the time.
When the hail stopped, he put the watch back in his pocket.
Twelve minutes had passed.
The ground was white with hailstones.
Not speaking a word, he drove to town
and canceled the new machinery he had ordered.

In the moment

Nearly 50 years ago, my father
gave a traded-work-day back
to a neighbor by helping with haying.
The neighbor's wife brought food out to the field
at noon-day, picnic style.
We ate beside mowing equipment
in open-air sunshine.
The smell of freshly cut hay curing on dry earth
mixed with fumes of gasoline
from our "H" and "M" International tractors.
The men talked farm talk,
while I concentrated on the plentiful supply
of breaded, fried chicken.
Even now I remember
the sky of that day (puffy, white clouds against the clear blue)
and chicken (sweet and juicy).

Class distinction

My mother said with a laugh
she married
beneath herself.
Back in the Dirty Thirties,
the family in which she grew up
always, at the least, had a supply of corncobs
to burn in the stove,
while my father and his brothers and sisters
burned dried cow dung
when the coal ran out.

Sitting with chicks

In the alfalfa fields of my childhood, prairie red-tailed hawks
liked nesting on top of last year's loose hay stacks
where, on summer days after following my father out to work,
I would pull my way up the sides,
grabbing the twiggy, crumbling stems,
digging my feet upward one step at a time.
The musty dust of old hay would sting my nose and eyes.
Reaching the lumpy, oblong top,
I would sit among half-grown hawk chicks
and the strewn-about litter of partly-eaten gophers and rabbits.
The chicks would be apprehensive,
but since they were as yet unable to fly,
could only edge sideways with a squawk.
The chicks' parents, on the other hand, with talons flashing,
on fixed wings would make low passes,
missing my head by a foot or two,
moving at great speed, making a whooshing sound,
turning about in the summer vaulted sky
of sunshine and floating columns of fluffy clouds.
After having satisfied my curiosity, I would climb down,
take my leave, and walk through the blooming alfalfa,
the sweet smell of purple and white blossoms filling my lungs.

Kittens in the rafters

Mama cat had placed her kittens in the safety
of our garage's overhead rafters,
nestled on a few flat boards spanning the two-by-fours.
There, the spotted-and-striped gray-black-and-white
babies mewed, eyes closed.
Mama cat didn't mind us little kids,
as she was our house pet,
unlike run-of-the-mill farm cats.
My older sister and I found a route
to the rafters of the garage by foot holds and pulls,
a route our parents never found out about.
But our very little, yellow-haired sister
could not make the climb.
So, by means of a five-gallon pail
and rope that was not much better than twine,
she was hauled up hand-over-hand to the
height of the rafters, her big, blue
and very wide eyes peering
over the sides of the tin bucket.
Either angels or just plumb dumb little-kids-luck
kept us safe as we perched, gathered around in
our baby kitty party.

The last load

My father and I mouthed out old cows
one November day
culling out the toothless ones.
He worked all day although
he wasn't feeling well.
He said he had pains.
He would not say where.
I said maybe we should quit
and do this another day.
He would not quit.
He just wanted the job done.
We sorted out the likely cows
and then ran them through the chute
where I mouthed out each one.
When the last cow was done,
he drove himself to town
and checked himself into the hospital.
He had been working with a heart attack.
Some men wait for God to intervene,
to tell them this one is the last load they'll lift.
My dad, after about a week,
went to his eternal rest.

Visions I sometimes see

I am in the wide open of prairie
as dawn breaks,
and earth still holds
the breath of night.
Far off on the grassy horizon,
herds of shaggy buffalo graze.
Their hooves roil dust clouds high
to the early light,
as fast, painted ponies carry saddleless riders
with bows and arrows closer and closer
to these beasts.
Behind, on foot,
far more ancient mammoth hunters
surround their prey, showing courage
as naked as their will to survive.
This brotherhood of those who came before
enacts an ageless dance
under the same open sky
I have come to know.

The land talks

The land talks to old timers
as turns of familiar roads replay
a younger day
over and over.
Like plows turn over land,
land turns over people,
making and shaping
from young
until gone.
For many of us, names are attached
not to gravestones,
but to land.

Mac

He rode the rails with tramps
in his younger days,
which might explain why
he never wore his wealth.
Occasionally I would see him at farm auctions,
looking nondescript,
wearing baggy, striped coveralls.
He usually stood over to the side of the sale ring,
not much of an expression on his face
except for his eyes that showed
he wasn't missing a bid,
or who was talking to whom.
Strangers paid him no heed, but
the locals knew what land he had
and he had more than most.
He was a lot like other older men
who were large land-holders –
most you couldn't pick out of a crowd
by the way they acted or held themselves.
Mac, like these others,
looked like a perfect fit behind the wheel
of his older, faded work pickup.
I couldn't help but marvel at this man
who'd had the insight
to buy and hold Coca-Cola stock
during the depths of The Great Depression
and never cash it in.

I know why

Close to a nearby road lies what once had been
a house's cellar and a barn's stone foundation.
The shelter belt running south from the foundation
is leafy and tall.
But to the north, trees are stunted and bare-branched.
Years ago, the last operator here
(a renter, not an owner)
kept blowing fuses in the barn's fuse box.
When he ran out of fuses, he used a coin, a nickel,
to close the gap.
It worked well, until the wiring grew hot
and started the barn on fire.
Wind was stiff from the south,
causing flames to leap to hundreds of hay bales
stacked along the north stretch of the shelter belt.
The hogs, barn, hay, trees fried.
Soon after that, with such bad luck, he gave up.
The house was sold and moved to a new location.

Grit

All the old ranchers in my neighborhood
have had one injury after another –
hobbled up feet, broken bones, knee replacements,
hernia repairs, shoulders torn out –
all from being blind-sided by charging animals,
swinging gates, falling iron and
dumb things that happen
when you're thinking of something else.
These guys have lifted heavy objects improperly,
slogged across foot-sucking mucky yards, step-by-step,
jarred their backbones countless times over rough terrain
because nobody else was around to do it,
because they had to,
because they did it yesterday,
because they are going to keep doing it until they can't.

Buster

What are you going to do,
on a fine fall Sunday afternoon
when you've been on the land eighty-plus years?
All your friends are either in the graveyard
or grown feeble and homebound, not worth a cuss.
What are you going to do,
but head outdoors
and fire the tractor up,
clean out the feedlot,
head to the fields,
and pile the manure up?
The good Lord might come a-calling
way too soon,
leaving your work undone.
On some days the aches and pains
might keep you inside,
but this day ain't one.
The land rolling under your tractor seat
is your domain.
There is no disputing on this fine fall day
who's the boss.

Derwood, what remains

On a wet morning,
Derwood's house made a big smoke.
The local fire station had been alerted
to reassure alarmed callers.
Even so, a few curious passers-by stopped
and were told the burn-down was deliberate.
Two generations before,
Derwood's grandfather had been an original homesteader.
His father had carried on husbanding the land.
But Derwood himself had, somehow,
let what he had fall on hard times.
His work over the years grew haphazard and rare.
His livestock generally fended for themselves.
Land taxes went unpaid,
published for all to see in the county newspaper.
A huge nest of broken down and obsolete tractors
collected from the area's farm sales,
surrounded his house.
Iron machinery sat wherever it got parked.

New acquisitions crowded each other,
spilling over broken-down fences,
grabbing the eye of even the most casual observer,
giving highway travelers a landmark.
Somehow, even as neglected as his place became,
Derwood hung on until old age
put him in a nursing home.
His lifetime collection was sold
by the ton
for scrap.
The flammable debris
remaining on the homestead
was piled around the house and then lit.
I could see a curl of grey smoke
from the blackened wreck of his house
for a week or better
when driving by on the highway.
Standing intact where the main bedroom had been
were the remains of a brass bed, open to the sky,
surrounded by ash.

The old ways

Amoz, one of the old timers,
asked me to work cattle on his place.
In a set of corrals showing some wear,
stood Amoz, chomping his half-smoked cigar,
holding in his hands a coiled,
very used horsewhip with whip-end frayed off.
Facing us was a pen of West River black-baldies
his renter bought.
My job was to sort calves from cows
and make the cows leave through a gate.
These range-running, unused-to-handling cattle
bounced off fence, ran helter-skelter
and having orneriness bred in,
were dangerous work.
An occasional cow would take
our urgings personally
and try to run us into the ground.
One lanky, wild-eyed beast took aim at Amoz.
With a lightening stroke,
he unleashed his horsewhip
and wrapping it around the cow's nose,
gave a yank.
The cow fell to her knees.
Meekly, she got to her feet and found the gate.
At the end, calves were sorted from cows.
Amoz, age 80, lit his stogie,
turned to us and said, "What's next?"

The gift

A wooden sign,
a foot-and-a-half long
by the-width-of-my-hand wide,
is fastened tight, head high,
under the eave next to my house door.
The letters are burnt in deep with a wood engraver,
neatly done, and clear-varnished,
letting strangers know who will answer the door.
The sign has kept well,
brought to me by my neighbor, Amos, who,
in his eighties, had stopped by one fall day, unannounced.
While chomping on his usual unlit, half-smoked cigar,
he'd immediately gotten me busy finding screws in my
shop
with which to secure the sign.
With that done, we leaned
over the warm hood of his ranch pickup,
and reminisced about jump-hunting ducks
together at local stock dams
and how the lay of the land
and the people he had known had changed.
From time to time as we talked,
we eyed the measure of our recent work
and decided the sign looked good where it hung.
I was, at that time,
half of Amos' age.
I didn't understand then,
but I do now – with that sign,
he meant for us to remember him.

Old money

The farmers and ranchers in my county
walk up wide, creaky wooden stairs of the County Courthouse
to the second floor twice a year,
like their fathers before them had done, and,
in most cases, like their grandfathers had done,
their calloused hands gliding
over polished wooden banisters.
Most wait 'til the last week to part with their money,
walking up to the County Treasurer's counter
a bit grim-faced,
just wanting to get an unpleasant chore finished and done.
Many wear hats and caps with a line of grime above the brim;
their eyes alert in sun-and-wind-weathered faces;
these folks work with their hands on a daily basis,
can tell you the mid-day commodity price quotes,
and pass judgment on the year by simply saying
it has been good or bad.
After they write out the check,
the County Treasurer passes back to them their receipts,
at which time, most make a little joke,
laugh, and say "Thank you,"
showing that how they feel is not
to be taken personally.

The starting-out years

As I was cinching up the rope on the gate
that leads to my pasture,
a thin young man in short-sleeved shirt passed by
in a cloud of dust on the nearby road.
Leaning forward, gripping the steering wheel
of a cab-less International tractor trailing a double mower,
he gave a quick wave in passing,
attention focused on the pebbly road.
The sun was on the edge of setting.
Behind him, a beat-up pickup followed,
lights flashing so it was sure to be seen.
Inside the cab was a lean young woman
hunched over the steering wheel, hair cut short,
eyes intent on following the dust up ahead,
husband and wife moving equipment around.
No doubt, they'll be up again early tomorrow,
racing the day to dark.

Jordan

On a day he was clipping bulls for presale,
smoothing their ragged hair coat,
one of the bulls got hurt
and lay down next to the feed rack.
Concerned, he walked over
and gave the bull a kick,
at which the bull jumped up in pain and rage,
promptly running him over.
He got away, a little shaken.
After another day of clipping,
he had a big gut ache.
Doctor said perforated colon
and began a long round of antibiotics
that eventually healed it,
but his back kept hurting worse.
Broken vertebrae, said the doc.
Surgery followed,
with opiates knocking back the pain.
Ten foot tall he felt,
until time came to wean off the meds.
He needed to stay at home and in bed,
with chills and shakes, sweating it out.
After two weeks, he was free.
He tells me this as he stands
next to the chute that holds cows
he makes his living artificially inseminating-AI.
Tough deal, this last four years,
he says.
Good wife,
is the credit he gives.

Early summer in production agriculture

Up and down on either side of roads,
the young and old, men and women,
pull loads every which way you look,
driving tractors hitched to various machines.
Mower-conditioners spewing green streams of alfalfa
followed in a few days by balers
dropping perfect cylinders of sun-dried crop.
They pull flatbeds containing tanks of water and chemicals
to service the spraying outfits that free the crops
of weeds and disease.
Down these same asphalt-coated, gravel-dusted back roads,
the men and women
haul cows to pasture with trailers and trucks,
haul bulls to pastured cows,
pulling loads on a time-schedule dictated
by an early-morning ringing alarm clock
and a sun that rises ever earlier
and ever brighter,
demanding all to produce,
to multiply
and be fruitful.

The hunter

While I was on my way to picking up a few alfalfa bales
with a loader and a bale carrier,
a stranger wearing an orange vest appeared,
seemingly out of nowhere,
walking along the right-of-way fence,
following two shorthairs sniffing
their way through unmowed grass.
No vehicles were in sight. I had the land
on both sides of the section line.
Who is this fellow? I thought as I
hopped out of my tractor.
"It's a beautiful day,"
were his first words.
I had to agree.
"Seen any sharptail grouse?
 I stirred some up a mile or so back,
but I think I lost them.
I'm seventy, and any day you can get up
and take care of yourself is a beautiful day.

Many in the world can't."
True, I thought.
"I don't really care whether or not I shoot a grouse.
I just enjoy being out here
in the grasslands."
We were miles from the nearest town,
miles from anyone at all.
At that point, I wished his hunt good luck,
now knowing what he was about.
I turned around to resume my work;
on second thought, I turned back to him.
I pointed out a quarter of land
another half-mile away and said, "That's mine over there.
Good grass. If there aren't sharptails in there,
you won't be likely to find them anyplace else."
Then I went back to my work
while the hunter headed to the distant grass
with his dogs,
both of us, in many ways,
alike.

Before eharmony

A woman
lost her husband.
They had homesteaded on the prairie,
far, far from any town.
She had little, but enough
to keep her tending chickens and cows,
although no children filled her days.
She grew lonely
as she watched tumbleweeds
bouncing and rolling forever.
One windy day, she tied a note
onto a big tumbleweed
that said: "Need Company?"
She set it free on a west-bound wind,
watching it race away and disappear
across unfenced land.
Weeks later, a trail-worn cowboy
stopped by, tipped his hat
while holding the note in his hand.
She sized him up,
maybe,
just maybe,
her shining knight.

South Dakota nice

A January in central South Dakota
that has record-breaking warm temperatures
makes for a landscape without snow.
The scenery looks familiar,
but not quite right.
Up in Mobridge,
the annual ice-fishing derby
cannot be held
because there is no ice on the river.
But it's held anyway, without anyone doing any fishing.
They draw for prizes and give them away.

Today's town square

You'll find men in country towns
nursing coffees at four-seater
rectangular tables in crossroads gas stops.
Their blue jeans and denim jackets
may be worn, but seldom holed or ripped.
Their clean work caps are set firmly on heads
with weathered faces.
Most have broad shoulders and deep chests
shaped by having made a living with their hands.
Each day they come in, pour their own cups,
pay at the counter, then sit pretty much in the same spot.
What they have in common is some idle time to spend,
either from retirement or from seasonal work slackness.
Back in their homes there is only television, whereas here,
almost everyone they know will eventually walk in.
Each time the door opens up, they note who comes and goes.
Comments about local news and weather
never seem to run out,
a routine that resembles days
when the storefronts all had sidewalk benches.

Blood ties

My cow ranch, like others, is held together with barbed wire
strung tight between posts enclosing 80 acres, quarters, sections,
miles and miles of razor-sharp barbs,
physical reminders to my cattle:
stay on my side of the fence.
I grew up following my father
checking fence, looking for breaks.
When fencing wire would dig into the palms
of my leather fencing gloves,
the firm recoil of its tensile strength let me know
that this was a job to grow into,
this repairing of fences, this maintaining of boundaries.
Occasionally, through haste or carelessness,
the steel barbs sliced my exposed flesh,
trickling red drops of blood from the jagged cut
to speckle my fencing tools
before falling to the earth.
I hardly notice anymore, these little nicks,
a small price to pay
for another tie that binds me
to what I've fenced in.

Family sayings

The five-foot iron bar
stuck point side down in the sod
by my son toppled over, striking my shoulder
as I knelt, head down,
tamping dirt around a fence-line railroad tie.
I wasn't hurt badly, just a bit of pain.
Unthinkingly, I said
"I wish you hadn't done that,"
the same words my own father used to say
when I had done something dumb.
As my son abashedly apologized
for his careless act,
I could but smile.
I could easily see my younger self
standing in his stead.
After all,
the bar had not hit my head.
Isn't a miss as good as a mile?

Insight

Warm south winds blow gusty,
even though twilight has come.
A yellow half moon hangs
in the southern quarter,
black dark still hours away.
By the calendar, frost is only
a day or two away.
Air smells of the earth
after months of growing and maturing.
On evenings like this, in my youth
I would sit outside feeling
relaxed and wise,
seeing the future
as though I was on one end of a long telescope
and the universal mysteries were on the other end.
Now, tonight, I dig with a long-handled shovel,
cleaning the muck out of a culvert so that
in the spring, water can drain,
trying to complete one more task
on this fall-shortened day.
My joints ache from the strain of repetitive motion;
upon completing the job, I am drenched in sweat.
In pale moonlight, I put away my tools
with damp muck still clinging
to my shoes and clothes,
feeling as though I am now
the connection between darkened earth
and moonlit sky.

The predictability of the unpredictable

While out working,
I heard about an approaching late-afternoon storm
on my tractor's radio.
The National Weather Service was telling listeners
to skedaddle to shelter,
which I did.
A third-inch of rain and some lightning came through,
just enough wet to stop work for the rest of the day.
Sitting in my house, I got a phone call from a neighbor
saying I had a stack on fire
in the field I had just left.
Hurrying back, I used a loader-tractor to remove
three flaming bales from the stack,
saving one of the bales
by stubbing out the burning end
like a cigarette butt

and then, using gloved hands,
pulling out the remaining fire.
Again, using my loader, I spread out
the other two bales that were too far gone to save,
spending an hour flipping the smoldering hay
over and over on the damp ground,
until only embers were left.
By that time, the sun had set.
I made my way back to the house,
my hair, cap, and work clothes reeking of smoke.
Above me, stars were glimmering
in the after-storm cleared skies.
The night air was rain-fresh.
A few hours earlier, I'd never
have been able to predict
this end-of-day's entertainment.

Tabernacle

Next to my garden
is a grey granite rock, waist high,
with rune-like rock ribbons
crisscrossing the surface.
It's big enough to use
for topping carrots and beets,
and tossing these greens and tapper roots
into nearby trees.
On this rock, I've washed melons and tomatoes
scrubbing the grit until they gleam.
My hands have planted them from seed,
hoed the weeds and watered and watered
throughout the thirsty summer,
just to get to this moment
where a slice of my knife removes the extraneous
of their once green life,
making them presentable
to neighbors, friends, and my own kitchen table.
May my rock table
always have a set of hands
after I am no longer able.

Rage against the dying of the year

On my usual sunset walk
along my usual dirt path,
black dusty soil puffs
at each of my steps.
I see the many little ways
autumn is advancing
quicker each day.
Alongside in the dust
are crickets and grasshoppers
at the end of their lives,
some upside down or sideways,
moving their limbs jerkily,
not giving up the fight.
Something in them still believes.
Tens of thousands of these once living
creatures, over the span of tens of
thousands of years, had their days
and summers in the sun
and, upon completion, returned to dust.
From this very same dust
that my feet step upon
shall come the miracle of spring,
the return of living green and all other things
that wiggle, crawl, walk and fly.

Not quitting yet

Tough winter – near-record snow.
Tough spring – more cold, more snow.
4th of July tonight – weatherman says
may be hail, high winds, even tornado.
I laid down 40 acres of hay
earlier today,
flat on the ground.
My having done that says something
to myself:
Not yet. No quit.

The Purpose:
With care
All things come to pass.

I planted a new row of evergreens
to back up an old shelter belt.
The old trees have grown thin
and broken-branched.
The new sprigs of juniper and red cedars
on a row of fresh-turned black dirt
make a scarce line of green
a quarter mile long.
The pine needles sticking up
above the ground six to 10 inches
every 10 feet or so,
the saplings are easy to overlook
unless you know what you're seeing.
With a little care and fair seasons,
five years from now
these baby trees will have grown
large enough to slow the snow
from sifting through downwind,
perhaps saving newborn calves
from a spring storm.
At ten years, these same trees
will be large enough
to stop even a stiff blizzardly wind.
At 30 years of age,
they'll be sheltering many creatures,
great and small.

One more chore before snow

My long-handled shovel
scrapes one-and-a-half-inch chip rock
out the back of my pickup box.
A spray of rocks fills a depression
that cattle hooves had trodden
next to a steel water tank
located in an isolated pasture.
The nearest neighbor is miles away.
Not yet 6 P.M. in mid-November,
twilight is gathering quickly,
becoming black, starless darkness.
My eyes are the sole judge
of the quality of my work.
I am the only one making sound
as the rock chips fall,
creating a few, brief, cold sparks.

Keeping faith

December in South Dakota
freezes ground hard like iron.
The deep-loamed soil that fuels our lives –
the reason we're all here –
is locked up, inaccessible, hidden,
buried in sleep,
forcing us to cope with only
the unyielding surface
and a far-away, meager sun.

When the frigid wind blows,
I feel unbound, rootless,
as though I may skid along
unanchored across my yard,
past my mailbox, down the road,
to send back postcards marked
Texas, Arizona.
Instead I choose to stay
where winter-whitened arms
will turn once again to summer bronze,
where my great-grandparents
once sat in their soddy,
day after day
after tending the few livestock they owned,
after shoveling the constant, recurring drifts
from their tar-papered door,
refusing to leave.

Occupational hazards

A general practitioner looked at X-rays of my neck,
the vertebrae outlined as whitish splotches.
"Did you know your neck is broken?" he asked,
as he stabbed a finger here and there on the chart
at what appeared to be splinters of bone
off-shooting from my neck vertebrae.
The doctor gave me a strange look,
as though to question why I was still standing.
This concerned me enough to seek a second opinion
from a more experienced doctor.
"Don't worry," he said,
"it's just calcification from old, forgotten injuries,"
the results of being in the path
of an occasional cow taking a shortcut,
the results of choosing not to earn a living
sitting behind a desk.

Conundrum

I'm getting sore of foot, thin of hair.
I've made a living from the dirt.
In the process, I've worn out more work boots
than years I've worked.
Few retire from ranching
by means other than dying or going broke.
Years ago, I laid out a plan of escape
to a longtime resident, telling him
I would find a sunny side of a hill
somewhere far from my working world
and spend my days contemplating
the eternal questions.
He said, "Sure you will. And you'll find out
that when you are there,
you'll be wishing you were here."

When they pulled up the tracks

My small town,
once made when the railroad came,
has quieted out
decade by decade.
House by house
falls down leaving only
crumbling foundations.

I am left with memories

A monarch butterfly
flutters barely off the ground
on a cleared-off lot
where my grandfather's house
used to stand.
Now there is only bare dirt where weeds grow.
I get my bearings from an old cottonwood tree
still standing, green-leafed on broken limbs.
It tells me where the sidewalk ran,
where the house used to stand.
I knew this place,
playing in every room
of a five-bedroom house
after church on Sundays,
holidays, any old day.
When I walked on through the front door,
never bothering to knock,
I was always welcome.
That's what family means.
But our own history
is a fragile thing
that falls away as those you know move on.
All I am left with is a lone cottonwood tree
to mark memories,
to show where earth reclaims earth.
Like the monarch,
it's time for me to move on.

Casting a line

The river rises,
the river falls.
The water changes,
time to move on.
The fish have gone
swimming in a different hole.

Hubris

Flat plains.
Vast emptiness.
Fill this earth!
Change this skyline!
But look!
The sky is always changing.
The earth is already filled.

On the plains

The breath of wind
harries far-away ocean waves,
hurls over mountain ranges,
comes to play unhindered on grass-stretched plains.
From the east, west, north, south,
it blows ceaselessly, tirelessly.
Wind seen in the form of clouds,
will-o'-wisps, whirlwinds, dust devils,
stirs at the first light of day.
Whispering, roaring, moaning, gusting,
rarely quiet,
wind talks in a tongue only natives,
the animals who live here,
understand.

My view

I need my view, the one out my window.
In the evening, no light can be seen from any neighbor's yard.
In the morning, rising dawn reveals
grass-textured sides of far off hills.

My sky

Above, a big bowl of sky.
Sunlight, starlight, clouds, snow, or rain,
the big bowl of sky remains.

Mesmerized by white

Nights are not just cold,
they are frighteningly cold.
Days are not much better.
Mornings, the sun slants so low
my eyes hurt from squinting.
Wind howls whenever a cold front
punches in from Canada, making ice crystals
out of yesterday's snow.

While I'm out doing chores

I can't stop myself
from watching snow will-o'-wisps
as they flow
southeasterly when northwest winds pick up.
I watch their drifting whiteness skitter
across flat ground, up hills, to disappear
as snow-fog on the horizon.
Today, a couple of emptied mineral bags
got away from me, caught by wind
to tumble after each other,
like coyote or dog pups playing.
They, too, disappear into the horizon
through dead prairie grass
and snow-fog.

A day in February

Yesterday, fluffy snow stood six inches level.
The grey sky and grey air corralled leftover warmth
from a February near-thaw.
Overnight, wind shifted to the Northwest
and a blow stormed through.
This morning, while feeding cows,
I cannot see beyond a hundred feet at times.
Between this wind and this cold, I doubt
whether a person, even warmly dressed, could survive
a mile-long walk. My cattle huddle
tight against the windbreaks,
knowing that, when the wind goes down,
feed is waiting just a short walk away.
I spend the afternoon moving snow from pathways
with my tractor snow-blower, fighting
against the building drifts.
At sunset, wind dies. Cattle go out to feed
and then come back to drink at the water tank.
Dark settles. I put my tractor into the machine shed
and walk over packed snow toward
my house lights.
What is left to do will wait for tomorrow.

In the dark of no moon

On a night black
as night can get,
my car lights catch the flash
of motion just below
the shoulder of the road,
running.
I am being paced by a coyote.
Side by side, for a few moments,
I race the hunter, my lights shining
off the tips of his back fur
as he bounds forward,
give him an almost ghostly appearance.
Then, with a tap on the accelerator,
I leave him to reunite
with where he belongs.

Not quite lunch hour

A big white jackrabbit emerged
out of a flurry of powdered snow,
hurling itself down a cow path.
Close behind, in hot pursuit,
followed two grey, winter-coated coyotes.
I was on my way
to check a water tank near a shelter belt
and was in direct line of the pursuers and the pursued.
The rabbit, his legs galloping,
passed my tractor without a glance.
The coyotes, seeing my tractor, slowed,
rocked one foot up, one foot down in indecision,
not sure of continuing.
I slipped a couple of bullets into a .22 rifle,
stepped outside the cab, and let go a shot
at the nearer coyote. I apparently missed,
but, at the gun's crack,
both took off at a blurring run,
abandoning their rabbit hunt,
leaving a trail of snow-fog
hanging low on a bright blue horizon
on this windless below-zero day.

Hungry time in early March

Open expanses of prairie are encrusted
by a foot or more of wind-blown snow
left over from a hard winter.
Daytime temperatures now climb into the 30's,
softening the surface of the drifts.
Rabbits still run swiftly atop them,
but coyotes sink in.
Mice and voles, usually an easy meal,
hide in tunnels between ground
and yet-to-be-melted icy roofs – unreachable.
Carcasses of many birds
which did not make it through
 lie frozen beneath the drifts – out of reach.
Now is the season
when thin, gaunt coyotes
walk into ranch yards, into house yards,
reaching for what might make
a meal.

Miscalculation

My cousin and I talk on the phone.
The snow is melting in South Dakota,
water running down draws and ditches,
shirt-sleeve weather on some days.
He is thinking of making the return north
in his RV, from Texas, as soon as he sees
a good stretch of weather.
I say, watch out
or you may be like the meadowlarks
who always seem to fly in
just before the last blizzard hits,
and I find them afterward
on the sparkling white snowbanks
next to my haystacks,
their sunshiny-yellow, speckled breasts catching my eye,
lying on their backs,
wings outstretched
and beaks pointing at the blue sky,
frozen stiff.

Vernal equinox

After a long, hard winter,
the land unlocks itself, pouring melt
into ancient, shallow prairie lakes
onto whose surfaces, huge rafts of Snows,
Great Canadas, Pintails, and Mallards gather,
the resting and the restless mixing together.
Distant, choppy waves
shimmer with movement
of wings taking off and landing
on freshly melted waters,
blue reflecting back blue sky.
Speckling the expanse,
silhouettes of returning waterfowl
promise the struggle against ice and cold
is done.

Change of seasons

First startling sight of spring
is jig-jagged,
a lightning bolt flashing down
from the blue-grey cloud skirting western sky.
With that comes the surprise
of water droplets
speckling this dry surface
where the wind hits.
Mud will cling to my shoes.
Seems like the seasons never change gradually,
but with a bang and a roar.

Magnificence

In the tall green graze
made from a good wet spring,
bulls, red and black,
lie deep in grass
resting from their task of eating all day,
each packing on pounds,
recovering from winter's frigid blasts.
When these one-ton-plus specimens
stand and stretch on long-limbed legs,
muscles are easily seen rippling
under taut summer-haired hides,
tails swinging at the occasional fly
and eyes alert, set in heavy, wide heads.
The bulls stand solid as the earth,
showing for all to see
how rain makes grass
and grass makes magnificent beasts
such as these.

Midsummer social

A few feet above midsummer purple-blossoming
alfalfa, dozens or perhaps hundreds
of half-dollar-sized,
solid yellow butterflies
flutter a floating dance,
waltzing across their flowering nectar lake
until, in a seemingly random meeting,
two butterflies circle each other rapidly
four, five, or six times,
then break apart to again float and flutter
until, within seconds, pairing with some other
half-dollar-sized, yellow flutter of wings.
They repeat this twirling,
spinning about madly
with another partner.

Cottontails

Wee bunnies in the grass,
lying in your mother's fur-lined nest,
stay still in the shallow dip
my lawn mower clipped open.
No longer hidden,
wide-eyed you are,
not much bigger than my thumb,
grey and brown flecked and striped,
noses a'twitching.
See those nearby cherry trees and lilacs?
In a few summer days
and a few hops,
you shall find
home anew.

Zen master

An antelope reclines in a newly-mown field
next to a hay bale,
eyes black, prong horns sprouted on his head,
legs tucked under himself, resting –
relaxed, but alert.
He gets up and walks,
content with his own company.

Dueling hawks

Windrows stretch
in long lines spiraling
around and around,
toward the center
as I bale prairie hay.
Everywhere, mice scurry
from under thick, raked western wheatgrass.
As my baler rolls up the cured green forage
several red-tailed hawks work the field,
swooping in wide circles
in a bright midsummer sky.
Frequently they plunge
toward ground, wings folded, talons out,
to clutch a clawful of the cut grass
containing a mouse.
Then, one hawk closely follows another's dive to the ground.
The first hawk lit briefly,
grabs a meal
and lifts immediately off.
The second hawk gives chase.
For hundreds of yards they tumble together,
the second hawk in a rage at losing out,
the first determined not to let go
of his mouse.
In tight circles,
they spiral
past my horizon.

Fate

An oncoming severe thunderstorm
rushes up from the horizon,
a sight of terrible beauty
from which you cannot turn.
You are at the mercy
of hail,
of wind,
of downpour ruining
the year's promised bounty.

Divine right

While working in hay fields
stacking bales,
I frequently find, at the tops of these round
three-quarter-ton cylinders of hay,
evidence they've been used as dining tables.
Disembodied legs of upland birds
and occasionally ducks,
macabre claws attached to leg sticks
are all that remain of these unfortunates
swept skyward in mid-stride
by a hawk plying his daily trade,
fulfilling his role
over the grasslands.

Transformer

Crouches
a prairie jackrabbit
in the hollow between tall grass
and a badger hole,
hidden
from sharp-eyed hawks
and sharp-nosed coyotes.
Nudged
from his nest by the nearing wheels
of my cattle-checking pickup, he hesitantly
creeps
his soft-furred body forward,
unsilhouetted, close to the ground,
ears back, pausing, intensely tense
as my wheels come closer, then
explodes
into a forty-mile-an-hour zigzagging run,
a grey streak into the grassy horizon,
gone.

The tells

In the July humid heat
of a plus ninety-degree afternoon,
the buck deer's massive velveted antlers
poked above the slough's sedge grasses,
looking like mossy forked tree branches,
out of place on a treeless prairie.
Come fall, after months of
polishing from rubbing
on fence-posts and brush,
he'll be ready to battle with fellow bucks
for his share of does.
For now he tries to stay hidden in his cover,
vulnerable, biding his time,
waiting for his rack to grow and harden.
But the rapid bobbing up and down
of his forked tines
as he pants from this heavy-heated
windless day, is giving him away
as he tries to stay invisible, motionless,
even though I'm a good fifty feet distant.
Quietly, I back-step and leave.

Homeward bound

A thirteen-striped gopher
ran down a cow path
very close to me,
running faster than one would think
four short legs could run.
He saw me,
stopped abruptly and flattened out,
belly to the ground,
black eyes glittering between bulging cheek pouches.
Tan fur with black stripes
camouflaged him to the earth.
I stepped back and returned to my task.
The prairie is big.
There is room for us both,
especially for those just wanting
to get home.

Flight of the monarch

In the ditches of our weedy, seedy
gravel roads,
the milkweed grows;
upon its leaves the monarch caterpillar feeds
and then undergoes
metamorphosis.
On clear fall days,
multitudes of orange and black wings
flutter, southbound.
Their offspring
will return
when the days lengthen,
following the scent of each other northward –
nectar-fueled travelers
fluttering a few feet
above a greening ground.

See ya

A flock of robins,
their breasts the color of rust,
land on my reddish-graveled yard.
Mid-October has been unseasonably cold.
The robins do skating hops
over the glazed ground and icy puddles
frozen from recent rains.
They eye this way, that way,
sideways, what was just recently mud,
but no earthworms wiggling
are to be seen.
All the robins can do is fly South.
Together as one bird
they lift off.

Premonitions

Red-on-black box-elder bugs bounce sideways
off the sunny side of my house
attempting to find the nearest foundation crack.
Pesky flies crawl about, rotating east to west
from one outside windowpane to the next
as sunlight arches overhead.
It's late October–cold is surely coming.
The bugs and I know it.
A night of killing frost will soon occur.
I feel gratitude for making it through
the season of work again.
Not until January will I think
cold, silent air
too quiet and too thin.

On windy fall days

I watch tumbleweeds go by
like little critters in chase
until they hit a fence.
There they stay,
just to strain and strain,
captured by strands of wire.
But out here when wind blows
one way,
soon it blows back
the other way.
Off again the tumbleweeds go,
playing their little games.

Timekeepers

An early cold front blows snow slantwise.
I'm fencing,
rolling up rusty barbed wire,
wig-a-wagging the stiff loop back and forth
on the snow-patched ground,
tearing out sixty-year-old fence
to make way for new fence.
The remaining shoots of green grass
seem out of place
on a day like this.
Overhead, geese appear in the V-shape
that puts their signature in the grey sky,
winging their way with the wind,
saying to me,
"Even if you try not to,
we keep track of time."

Falconers

On the frozen, snow-covered prairie,
golden eagles and red-tailed hawks
perch patiently at the tops
of tall, creosoted poles next to highways,
keenly watching
Tahoes, Explorers, and eighteen-wheelers
flush deer, jackrabbits, grouse, and pheasants
foraging on the shoulder
onto the black asphalt.
Occasionally, red brake lights flash
and then, through thin air,
the audible thump of vehicle connecting
with prey.
The birds, when hungry, rise windward
and then, in long swoops, descend
to their winter's game trail
to retrieve and feast.

Winter solstice

The dark of the year creeps up
gradually, almost unnoticed,
in the northern plains.
The cold that is always lurking
in the northwest wind blows in
locking up the ground with biting frost.
A great stillness settles in.
Every track in snow
leads to a solitary story
of a beating heart, a faint fog
of breath that sits quietly
in a clump of stiff grass, a sheltering hollow.
I stand in the early blackness of night,
no longer separated from the distant
planets or stars by warmth or light:
I am no different
from any of God's other creatures
who are waiting out the dark
of a dying year.
"I am," I say.
I will wait for the return of light.

Worth getting up for

In winter, overnight fog freezes thick.
Early morning light shows frost
as white shadows upon white shadows
until strengthening sunlight
transforms all into diamond glitter.
By noon,
just wet, drab, everyday earth remains.

Cattle work

The cows stand quietly
on a thin soup of slop
in an iced-over cattle yard.
Noonday sun peeking out
from thin high clouds
gives their thick, winter-hided hair
a shine.
Temps pushed 40 degrees,
with barely a breath of wind,
a rare day for usually bitter cold January.
In near silence, cattle chew
their cud, waiting their turn
to be given midwinter
pre-calving vaccinations.
With a wave of hands and a holler,
every few minutes
another small bunch are urged
through the crowding pen
into the chute.
After a couple sharp pokes with needles,
the cows scramble out from the gate,
another step closer
to birthing healthy spring calves.

Early spring, genesis

The setting sun glows orange-red,
fading upward into the darker blue.
Coming night, though, a newly-full
yellow moon rises in the eastern sky.
Early spring air hangs at 50 degrees,
with the temperature dropping.
I walk coatless,
across a cattle-filled yard,
cattle so used to me they barely stir.
I just delivered a live calf,
leaving him warm and still wet
on a bed of barn straw
so that he and his mother can get acquainted.
There is not a breath of breeze in the air,
as though all of creation
is taking a pause.

The near and the far

At the first of dawn
four newborn, healthy calves
rested among my two-year-old cows.
Penned in the yard,
the first-calf mothers stand attentively,
noses toward their babies.
A bare hint of frost laces the ground.
Rising sun in the east
washes the sky a rose-red.
From the south, lines of snow geese
flash white, wing their way north.
Not a cloud
nor a stir of wind
separates what is near
from far.

Empty nest

I put the fiberglass cane away,
the calving chains hang resting on the barn wall,
the calf puller has found its corner,
the nursing bottle and iodine jug are stowed
back in the basement with the med kit.
The hayrack sits alone with its last half-eaten bale.
Today, the last pairs were loaded up
from these calving yards and delivered
to their summer, green pastures.
As I open the trailer doors, the cows don't give
one look back; their noses trail close to the ground,
sniffing fresh, new grass,
bawling for their calves to stay near,
unaccustomed to this unfettered,
uncorralled, open-skied domain.

Freed from my daily care, freed from fear
of hearing the weatherman report, "Another big-time low
heading this way," bringing calf-killing
snows or cold rains,
I'm done with the frantic, confusing,
bringing-a-troubled-cow-in-from-the-dark;
done with the whole wet,
bawling, kicking, dangerous, sliding-around-in-the mud-and-manure-
attended-births-and-sometimes-deaths
wonderful mess.
No longer will the first and last thoughts of my day
be about cows and calves.
I'm done with the constant walk from house
to barn to yard and back to house.
Done with it all for another year, as I pass by
my once busy yards, now with only a fly or two buzzing about –
mighty quiet, now.

Calving log book

Lost two cows from hardware disease.
One cow paralyzed from calving–down 3 days, then back up.
Two calves died from pneumonia.
Five calves died from being stepped on,
either in the barn pens or outside in mud.
Eleven calves died from birthing difficulties.
One calf died from a busted gut.
Eight calves died from other miscellaneous reasons.
Ten cows had twins.
I swapped ten calves, from cows that either had
twins or were too old,
to cows that lost their calves.
Three cows had bad mastitis.
I was struck twice by irate cows
and totally run over once, resulting in
broken glasses and a sore neck.
I worked in knee-deep mud and record cold.
Still, the grass greened early.

sold → 396
—4
392

Calved 392 cows

first calf March 24 — cold
Last calf May 30

All cows out to pasture
May 30 — muddy
Turned out bulls June 25

A dirty job

Two months before turn-out time,
the Black Angus bull had been a fine one-ton specimen
of hide, muscle, and bone – a crucial partner
in the processes that make this ranch operate.
Sometime during the first week or two after turnout,
a bit of bacteria lurking in the ooze
of a muddy hole slipped into a crack in his hoof
and started up a bad case of foot rot
that quickly worsened, infecting his joints.
The round after round of antibiotics
injected into his hind end
did little good.
Even though fed and watered by my own hand,
he grew constantly thinner and weaker
until, one morning, although prodded,
he couldn't muster the strength to gain his feet,
a sure sign his end was near.
Shooting a sick bull with a high-powered rifle
probably sounds like a cinch,
but seems to be a job that always takes two shots
because the skull is so thick.
I find myself saying, "I'm sorry,"
as I touch off the rounds.

Of men, mice and fence fixers –
they often go awry

My fencing pincers wandered off
and got lost this spring
as I repaired broken barbwire T-post fence.
Usually I have them shoved in my rear pocket,
ready to work when needed.
I looked in the pickup box,
I looked in the pickup cab,
walked around the pickup
carefully looking
in short spring grass.
I walked down fence
where I had used them last,
wrapping wire staples around B-wire
to hold them fast to T-posts.

Then I looked again
in the pickup, around the pickup
and again, up and down fence.
Patting my pockets,
right to left, front to back,
I finally concluded on
this early May Sunday morning,
my pinchers have been raptured
and gone to barbwire heaven,
where wire always cuts soft
and never breaks when stretched or wrapped.
After this conclusion and thinking
about effects of one long day after next
of a done and gone calving season,
it was time to head home
and take a nap.

Doctoring

About July the sick calves
start showing up out in the pasture,
brought on by the warm weather, flies,
or just the spring vaccination shots wearing off.
Rash of calves with droopy ears,
snotty noses, dull eyes
and hanging heads.
Who really knows why?
Serious stuff though,
these makings of an outbreak
where big strong calves get weak
to the point of lying down to die.
The first sign, if not an already dead calf,
is a calf off by himself not looking right.
Then, in quick order of a few days,

the contagion runs
through what represents your entire year's paycheck.
Some call it dust-pneumonia, shipping fever.
The vets call the disease Pasteurella.
Some years you're lucky and the bug
passes your herd by. Other years
you're unlucky.
Those who can rope, rope the sick ones
one by one, and treat them with drugs.
Others get CO2 guns
and shoot them with a dart full of antibiotics.
I'm not much good at either.
I run my calves from the pasture
into a pen and pull off the sick ones
and treat them at close quarters
with the jab of a needle,
hoping the medicine will turn the dull,
sick eyes bright in a couple days.

Hobby

A cow carcass in a pasture,
like a shipwreck on a beach,
testament to an untimely end.
The arch of ribs
shows up big, white silhouetted
against the ground
before years settle what remains
deeper into the earth.

I knew an older guy
whose every fence post
on both sides of the driveway
leading up to his house
was topped by a cow skull.
Years picking them up
and bringing them back home.
A whole herd of vacant eyes,
weather-whitened bone, and bovine teeth
lined up silent, facing visitors,
seeming to insist no matter
what fortune or weather would bring
to his ranch,
these would keep him company.

Dawn's early light

When the rooster crows
at first light of day,
letting the sun know who's boss,
he also lets the fox know
where the chickens are.

Summer canvas

Summer, on prairie never farmed,
wild flowers bloom –
spots of yellow,
spots of blue,
spots of white,
spots of just about every color.
Wild flowers
stand tall above the grass,
or peek through its blades.
See little flowers down near grass
roots,
no bigger than a mouse's ear.
Say to Van Gogh,
if he were here,
"Paint, if you can,
what we already see."

"Stop, hey, what's that sound,
everybody look what's going down."

For What It's Worth
Written by Steven Stills,
recorded by Buffalo Springfield, 1966.

A moment of requiem for the prairie

Sod, whether turned by a plow
or killed the modern way
by chemicals,
takes a long time to rot down.
The roots are tough,
like ends of frayed ropes.
Slowly they crumble,
exhaling carbon.
Along country roads
where grasslands have been freshly converted,
this interlude must be waited out
before new crops can be planted.
The dead prairie sits,
silent,
a graveyard.

Bread basket of gamblers

In the land of John Deere, Case IH,
Caterpillar, Monsanto, New Holland and Cargill,
the big names place ads
in traditional and online media
to woo anyone
who has a half million or more to spend.
Giants of industry pitch
heavy-duty, cast iron, molded plastic,
tech-stuffed agricultural production marvels
to folks who wear denim jeans and seed caps.
All calculate
cost and profit.
Those who sell and those who buy
know what they are doing is in historic transition,
hanging both on the whims of nature
and on the unpredictable nature
of global international trade.

Harvest on the high plains

Herds of behemoth combines
followed by gravity cart tenders
roam dirt section-line roads
en route to the gathering of corn.
Fleets of semis bearing tons
of modern-day miracle maize
deliver their tribute to
small-town elevators –
shiny, silver-cylinder
granaries crammed
until they can hold no more.
Overflowing abundance
nurtured by what was
once native prairie buffalo grass,
is heaped high on the ground,
yellow mountains reaching for the sky,
remnants of buffalo bones, buffalo fat –
an unburnt offering, waiting.

Market analysis from a tractor seat

The news, out in the country,
wasn't good in early fall of '08.
Order buyers sat in the top row
of the cattle auction barns,
hands folded,
order cards in shirt pockets, unmarked,
watching the few cattle coming in,
walking out,
barely bid on
by the local feedlots.
Buyers' cell phones weren't ringing,
everybody on the other end glued to monitors
watching
the Dow Jones and the Chicago commodities
erratically drop.
Word was out –
some damn fool somewhere, somehow,
using someone else's money,
had bought and sold a cow,
a barrel of oil, a bushel of wheat, a mortgaged house,
a serialized derivative
one time too many
without ever actually owning what he had sold.

Rural conversion

Crop lines trim right up to the waterways,
courtesy of effective chemical sprays.
Genetically-modified, drought-resistant
soybeans and corn run up to the edges of creeks
and over hills, GPSed and no-tilled.
Drain-tiles drain lowlands,
and lowlands give no water back to wetlands.
The wetlands are now the drylands
which become cropland.
The only native grass to be found
is in old, untrimmed country cemeteries
near the small towns, the gone towns.
That is how death of grassland spreads,
one technological advance at a time.

A funeral lament

As I shut a pasture gate, miles away from home,
a neighbor pulls up.
After exchanging the usual greetings, I ask him what
brings him down this particular road,
a road neither he nor anyone else lives on.
He says he's coming back from a funeral in town,
and has heard that the pasture land across this road
has been sold and is going to be broken up, big time.
He thought he would take a look if they have gotten started.
I know the previous owner of this land.
He had said a while back he would never sell.
"Well," says my neighbor, "if you had been offered
the price they were offered, you might have sold, too."
I look across the road as he talks:
acres of rising and falling
swells of grass
soon to be put to the plow.

The grubs, the bugs, the living sod
and all the wildflowers alive
in this continuous grass, this fragment of what
once was a never-ending carpet called The Great Plains,
will soon be dead.
"Oh well," says my neighbor,
"can't blame 'em for breaking good pasture.
The way economics are, cows won't pay
what that land cost."
I know that corn and wheat will feed many people.
People, by and large, are a good cause.
Still, I wonder as I drive home
on a dusty country lane,
who will pay to keep
the crickets and the bumblebees,
the prairie's food chain
few ever get to see from disappearing?

Trends

Surrounded by rows of corn,
the dark blue Harvestore silos stand tall,
no longer connected
to where the feedlots used to be,
the fences, feedlines, and loading pads torn out,
gone, smoothed over.
Cattle were too much work
and the money wasn't there.
Instead,
silvery, big-bushel bins
cluster around a cement-padded dump
where thousand-bushel grain trucks are weighed,
unloaded, and their content sent with a whoosh
down and up interconnected legs to a bin,
to wait for a Chicago/China/inter-global trade,
transportation arranged by truck, barge, or train.
From the highway or up close, it's obvious
we're just getting a handle on the change.

Change comes to East River, South Dakota

Stones, rocks,
boulders the size of pickup trucks,
ripped out, backhoed
and buried into the once grassy hillsides
from which they, glaciered, came
fourteen thousand years ago.
This land flattened,
smoothed over by tons of heavy, machined land rollers
that readied the black soil for fields
of row crop corn and soybeans,
goes everywhere from horizon to horizon,
right down to the pot-holed water's edge
where scarcely even a cattail grows.
Round Up chemicals have taken out
just about every weed.
Each available acre is cash crop,
with no room for a bird, for a bee,
for a wild flower or tree.
All this used to be grassland
where song birds sang and butterflies cocooned.
There is not a cow, not a cowman,
for miles and miles on the grain-truck-pounded highways.

Lonesome blues of a John Deere cowboy

He's a cowboy
wearing a black cowboy hat,
riding high
on an oil-cushioned hydraulic tractor seat,
bouncing in the cab of a John Deere
green machine,
pulling a rock picker across
a just-gleaned soybean field,
beating in rocks
with revolving rock-reel arms,
listening to country tunes,
singing along to
"Someday soon,
someday soon
I'll be there with you."

Somewhere over the horizon

There are not enough places
where cowboys are,
where grass sticks up,
and fences stand few and far.

Bruce Roseland

Finding a way

By fall the grass that grew thick
in my pastures has been clipped
close to its roots by cattle,
leaving stubble
like the bristles of a brush.
Cows have stamped
narrow paths through what grass is left.
These cow paths seemingly meander,
leading around, not over,
holes and rocks.
If followed they will converge
at water holes.
There is order in the cattle's domain,
just by them being who they are,
making prairie into pasture.
I too am engaged in work
that turns nature to my own use.
I cannot stay unless
what I do feeds me.
If you were to follow me
on many of my days,
you would think my path, too, meanders.

The profane and the sacred

But as I have lived my days,
working in the rise and fall of land
that sweeps to sky,
from sunrise glow to night shadow,
somehow, I sense the sacred in the ordinary.

The stand-outs

My cows pretty much look the same,
the result of years of buying all black Angus bulls.
But I still have those cows
with individual markings,
throwbacks to years ago crossbreeding,
a spot of white
on a face or throat, or a curly swirl of hair.
These I notice, and keeping track
of their life histories
is a bit easier than for all the other cows
who are distinguished only by a numbered tag.
I find myself cheering a little when these
uniquely-marked cows, in the fall, are pronounced
"pregnant" by the vet,
because they'll stay another year
and hopefully drop a live, healthy calf.
And in the spring, I catch myself smiling
a bit as I realize this isn't merely a business
of dollars and pounds of beef.
I find myself rooting for the individual.

I feel the pull of another year

Light drizzle is coming down,
puffing on an easy wind,
just enough to let you know it's wet.
A thermometer tacked on an outbuilding wall
says 50 degrees, the start of cooling toward winter.
Fall run of calves has begun
at the local livestock auctions,
meaning money in the pocket,
rewards reaped from that hard, cold, wet spring
we all went through.
Possible calf losses loomed each day,
the muck was deep and the odds didn't
look very good.
Still, months later, on a morning like this,
when damp cool is in the air,
my thoughts drift forward,
just like the seasons changing,
turning toward a new year.
I'll be drawn again to check on life
being born in the lots,
making sure nothing has gone wrong.
I'll eagerly wait for a calf's first gasping breath,
and those wobbly first steps on legs newly outstretched,
instinctively nuzzling toward
the warmth of a waiting mom.
I see myself there, part of this scene,
wet wind on my face, hunkered in my work clothes,
the scent of earth and sky, cow and calf, in the air.

First snow

First snow falling soft
on autumn grass
leads the eye
to where sky blends into earth.
All is white except for cattle
still grazing pasturelands,
heads lowered, nuzzling down deep,
seeking the last hidden green
of summer.
Snow sits lightly upon their dark backs.
Behind them, hoof tracks
weave pock marks that fill with shadows.
Yet-to-be-weaned calves
trail close to their mothers' sides.
They take a few steps, and then a bite,
getting all the good
they can find.

Hard winter

Another day of snow blowing
at minus 50 wind chill,
frightening in its fury.
The last thaw was five weeks and two feet ago.
This powdered, feathery snow just shifts and snakes along,
turning into hard drifts.
In miles of white, nothing living moves.
All around me, the landscape is devoid of life,
except for the few acres of my buildings, haystacks and cows.
As the sun rises, the wind comes up,
making any skyline an indefinite, hazy white.
I judge how bad it is
by what familiar landmarks can or cannot be seen.
We are both a hardy and foolhardy lot.
Pickups, semi-trucks and cars can occasionally be seen
driving down roads, even though
DOT has declared a "No Travel Advisory."

Business of the day still has to go on.
So, each morning, after coffee and a look out the window,
whatever needs to get done, gets done:
kids to school, groceries to buy.
For me, cattle need to be fed.
Some of my neighbors are already calving.
I feel for them.
My season is a little further off.
I try to push snow out of yards,
preparing a spot for a calf to lie down.
I worry about running out of places to push the snow,
trying not to block gates and pathways.
I tick off one more day of winter,
doing my best to remind myself of the good
that moisture lying on the ground brings,
feeding grass that will come in spring.

Pasque petals

In early April, while I'm checking fence,
repairing winter's damage, readying pastures
for the summer's grazing yet to come,
purple pasque flowers
on their pale green stalks
sprout amidst winter's deadened grasses
as little surprises – almost-hidden
bits of vivid color.
These flowers bloom
on the same ground year after year.
They have most likely always been here.
While exploring grassy stretches near my home
as a young child, the sight of this first spring flower
poking through stony hillsides startled me –
so delicate, so purple, so alive –
growing in the season when prairie potholes
fill with snow-melt.

With the Easter story fresh in my mind,
I had proof of the resurrection of the prairie
after our usual drawn-out winter.
I would pick a few and take them home
to my mother, knowing I carried
a sure sign of the return of life.
Each year they faded, and the cattle grazed,
trampling upon their ground.
I would look and wonder where they had gone.
I know now that underneath my feet,
these flowers wait;
they will do again what they have done
for countless springs,
saying with purple petals
that whatever else may come and go,
as long as there is native sod,
they shall be the first to herald the warming sun
which stirs new life.

On some days, I'm already there

Morning arose like a cathedral
as I drove down a lightly-traveled country road
from one late fall chore to the next,
a skim of grey-blue clouds overhead;
to the east, turquoise sky.
The sun, not yet breaking the horizon,
shone stained-glass-ruby light.
Cattle grazed across fenced pastures,
pulling fall-rain-greened grass into contented mouths,
their yet-to-be-weaned big-bellied calves
keeping pace alongside them.
Because of the cooler weather,
their tails were no longer continuously swatting flies.
Flights of Mallard ducks rested in small, scattered groups
in shallow roadside ponds, the males' green heads
and the quieter browns of the females mixing in a slow,
paddling dance on weedy waters.
Weathered brown bales were scattered across hayfields,
packages of summer waiting to be moved to stockyards.
The light of the new day climbed with each mile I drove,
touching the highest clouds and sky with a white-rosy shine;
I imagined
if I were to be released from my own eventual rest
and come back to this day,
I would think this paradise.

On any clear night

Standing outside in my yard,
living as I do away from all light
that people make,
the ground on which I stand fades outward,
dark, flat and formless,
until night sky sweeps upward
in a blaze of white, yellow and red
star sprinkles,
a solid, curving wall, an infinity of suns.
From this darkened earth,
I fall skyward,
heaven bound.

Seek

Seek the grasslands
rolling out to horizons unbound.
Seek where you shall find
the full-cut measure of your character.
Seek where, if you put down roots
and are tenacious,
you will find a way to survive.
Seek where a lone tree can stand tall,
holding a multitude of history.
Seek where the earth and you are one.

Bruce Roseland, Seneca, SD

Bruce Roseland is a fourth-generation cattleman who grew up on a ranch in north central South Dakota. Roseland is the author of *The Last Buffalo,* 2006 (2007 Wrangler Award), *A Prairie Prayer,* 2008 (2009 Will Rogers Medallion Award), *Church of the Holy Sunrise,* 2012, *Song for my Mother,* 2014, *Gift of Moments,* 2016, and *Cowman,* 2018 (2019 Will Rogers Medallion Award). *Heart of the Prairie* (2021), Scurfpea Publishing, Sioux Falls, SD, is Bruce's seventh book of free verse poetry. Roseland received a B.A. (1974)/M.A. (1980) in Sociology from the Univ. of North Dakota. At age 28, he returned to the land, a place that made sense to him in a world that frequently does not. Roseland is President of South Dakota State Poetry Society and a SD Humanities Scholar. Bruce still works his family ranch outside of Seneca, South Dakota.

Made in the USA
Monee, IL
31 May 2021